Bride

bride's
Maid

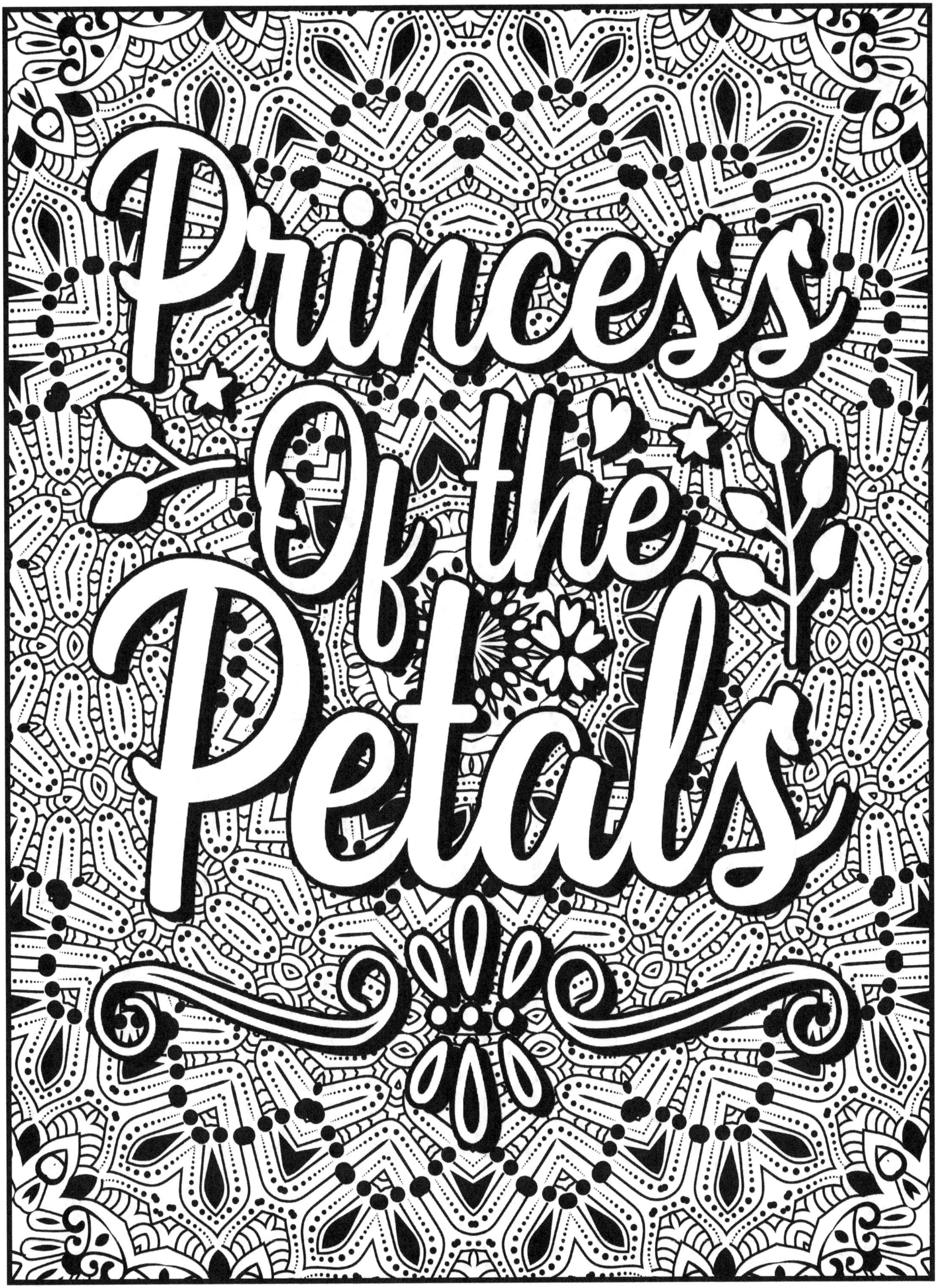
Princess
Of the
Petals

never
too old
to be a
BRIDESMAID

mother
of the
groom

mother
of the
groom

mother
of the
groom

mother
of the
groom

Mother
OF THE
Bride

Mother
Of
Honor

Matron
OF
honor

Marry
Me

man
OF
honor

maid
OF
honor

JR
brides
maid

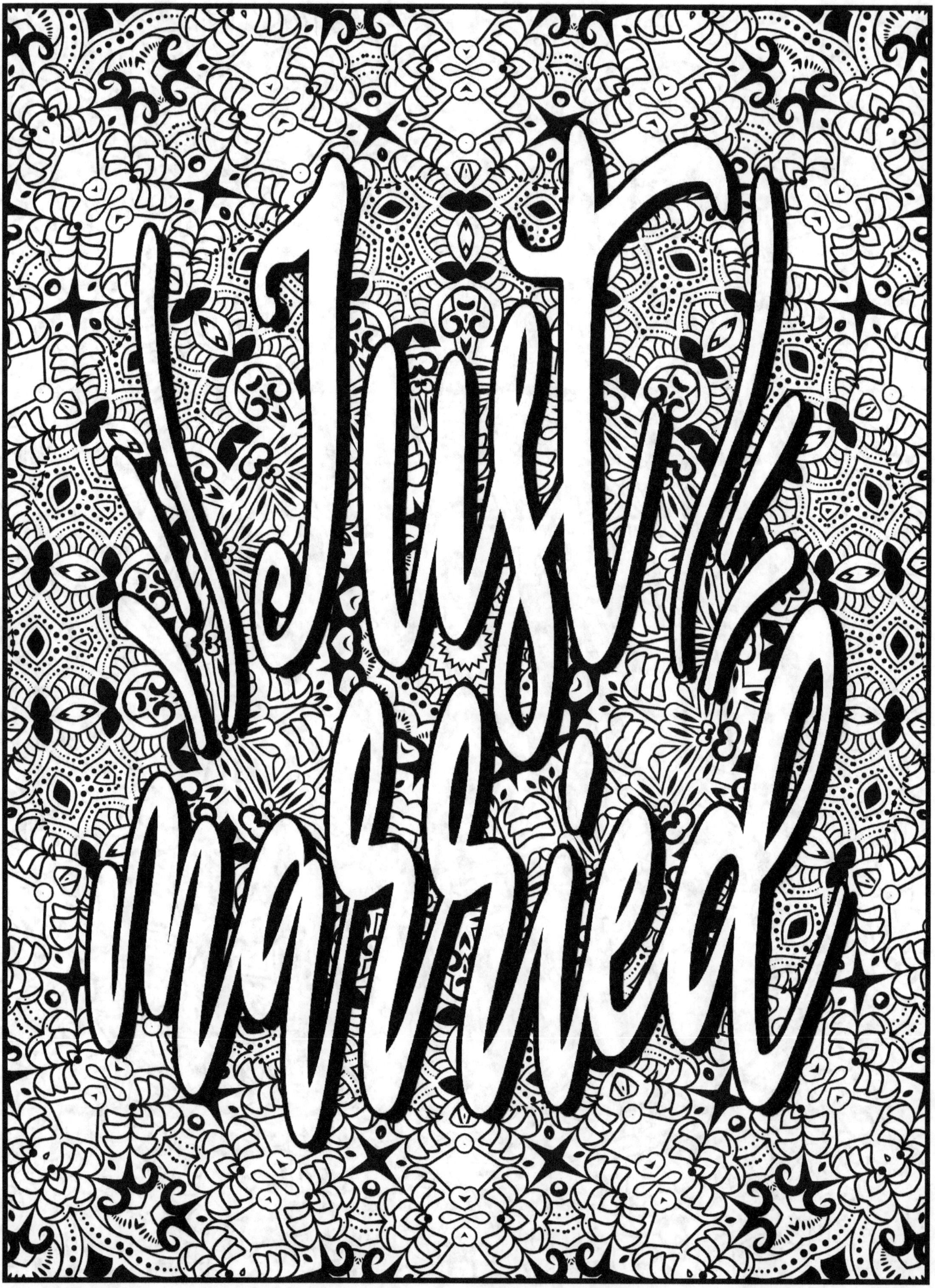
Just
married

I said
yes

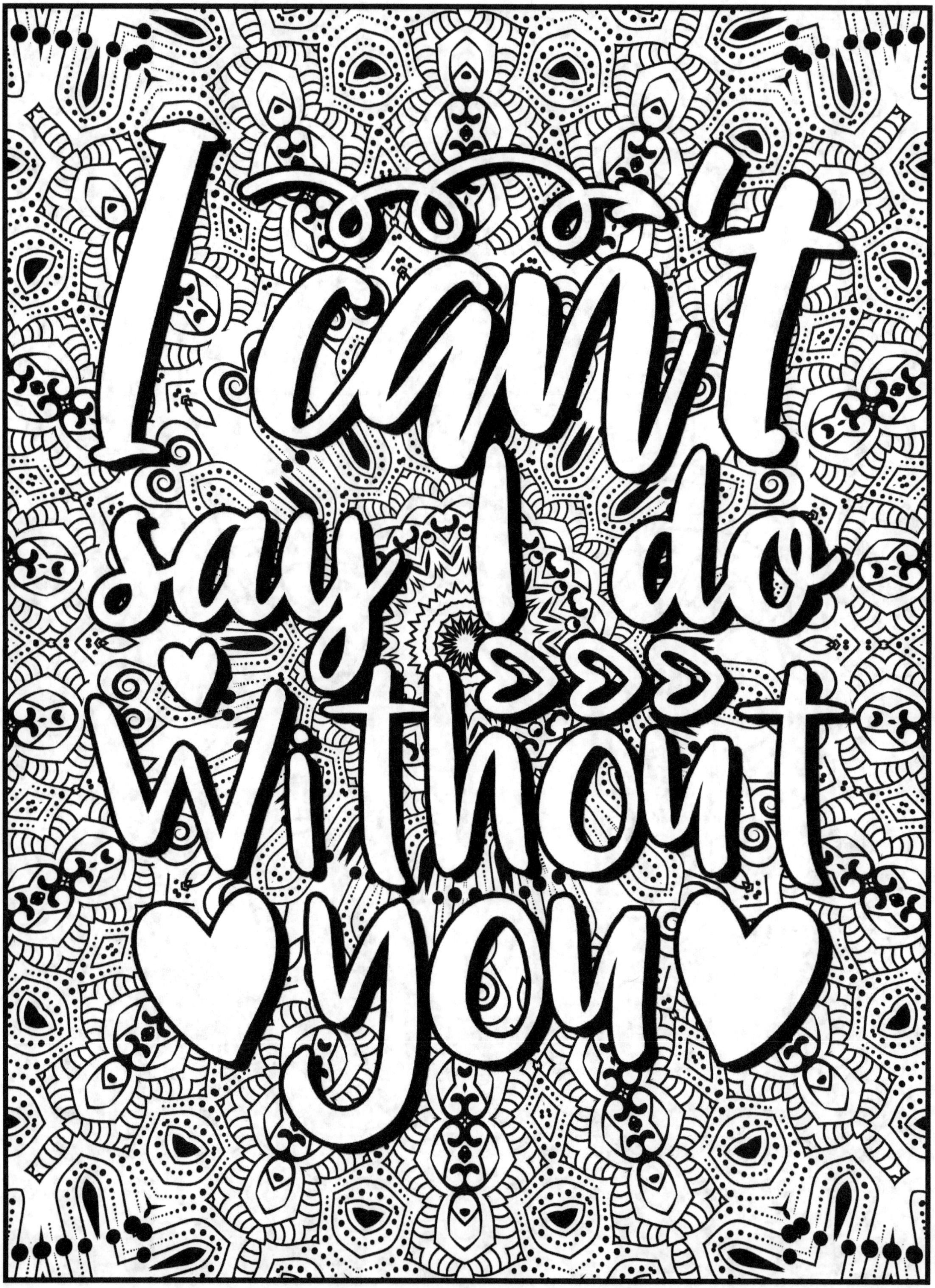
I can't
say I do
without
you

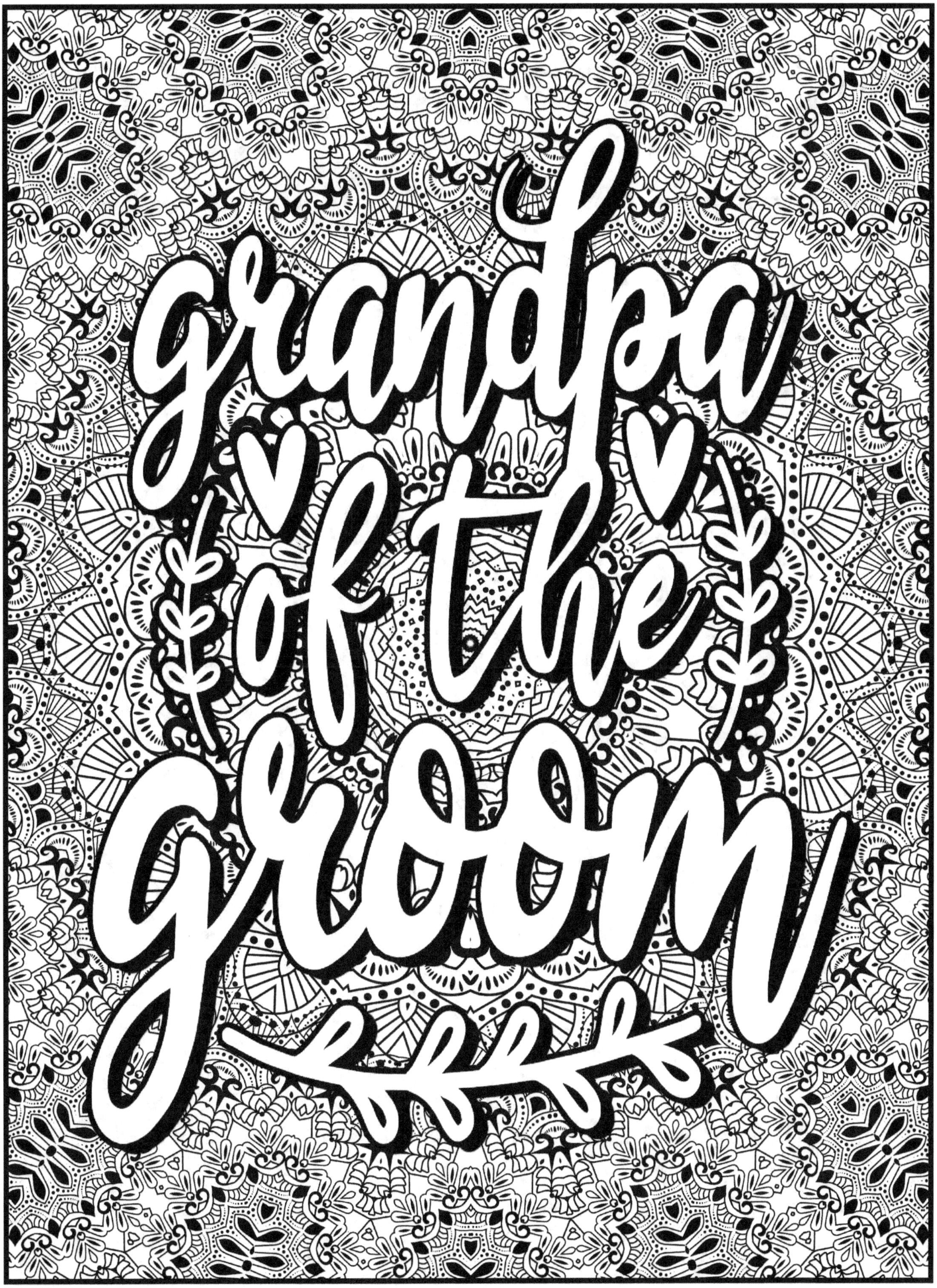
grandpa
of the
groom

grandma
of the
bride

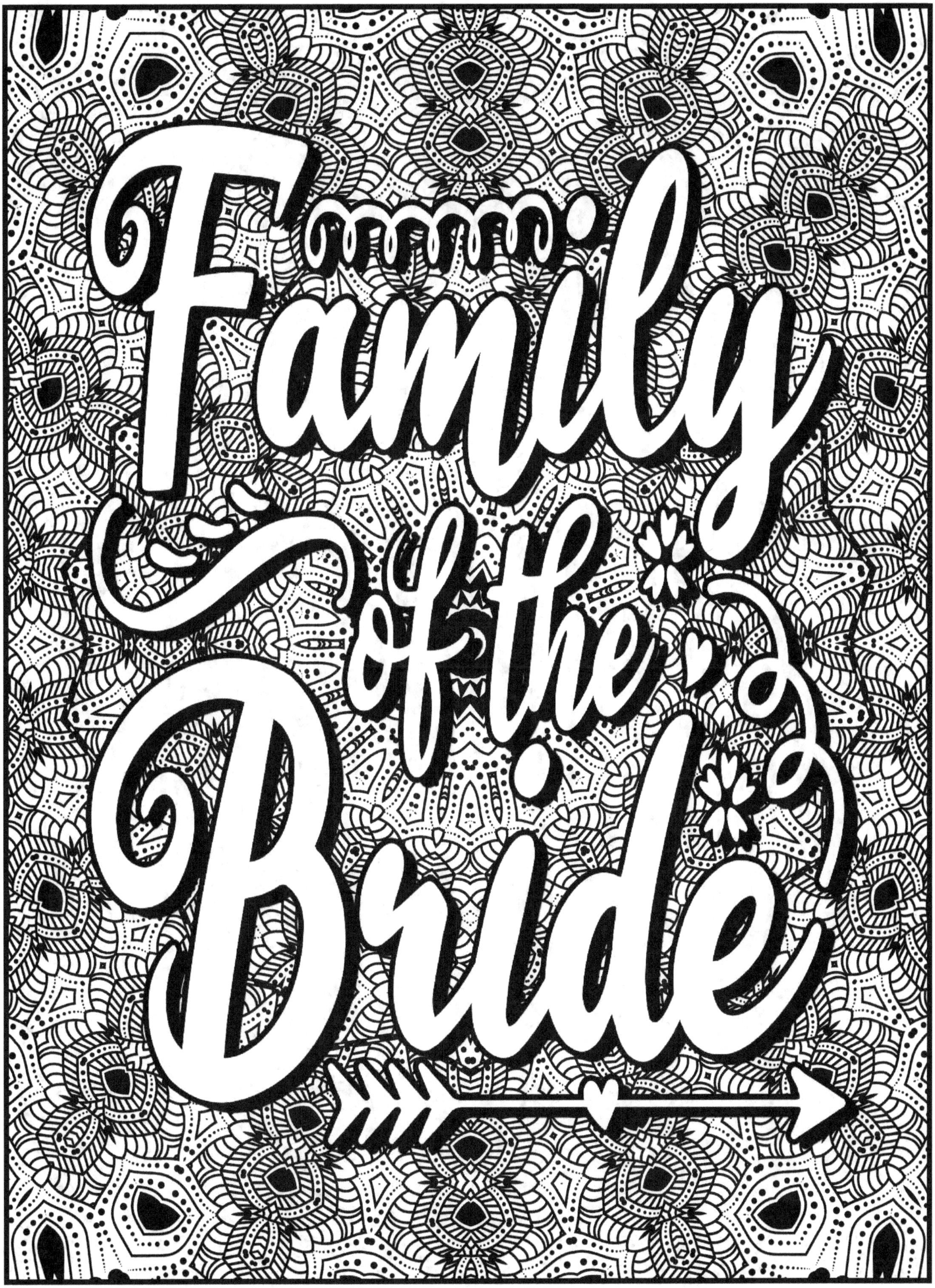
Family
of the
Bride

Engaged

Chaos
COORDINATOR

POP
fizz kiss

Page Boy

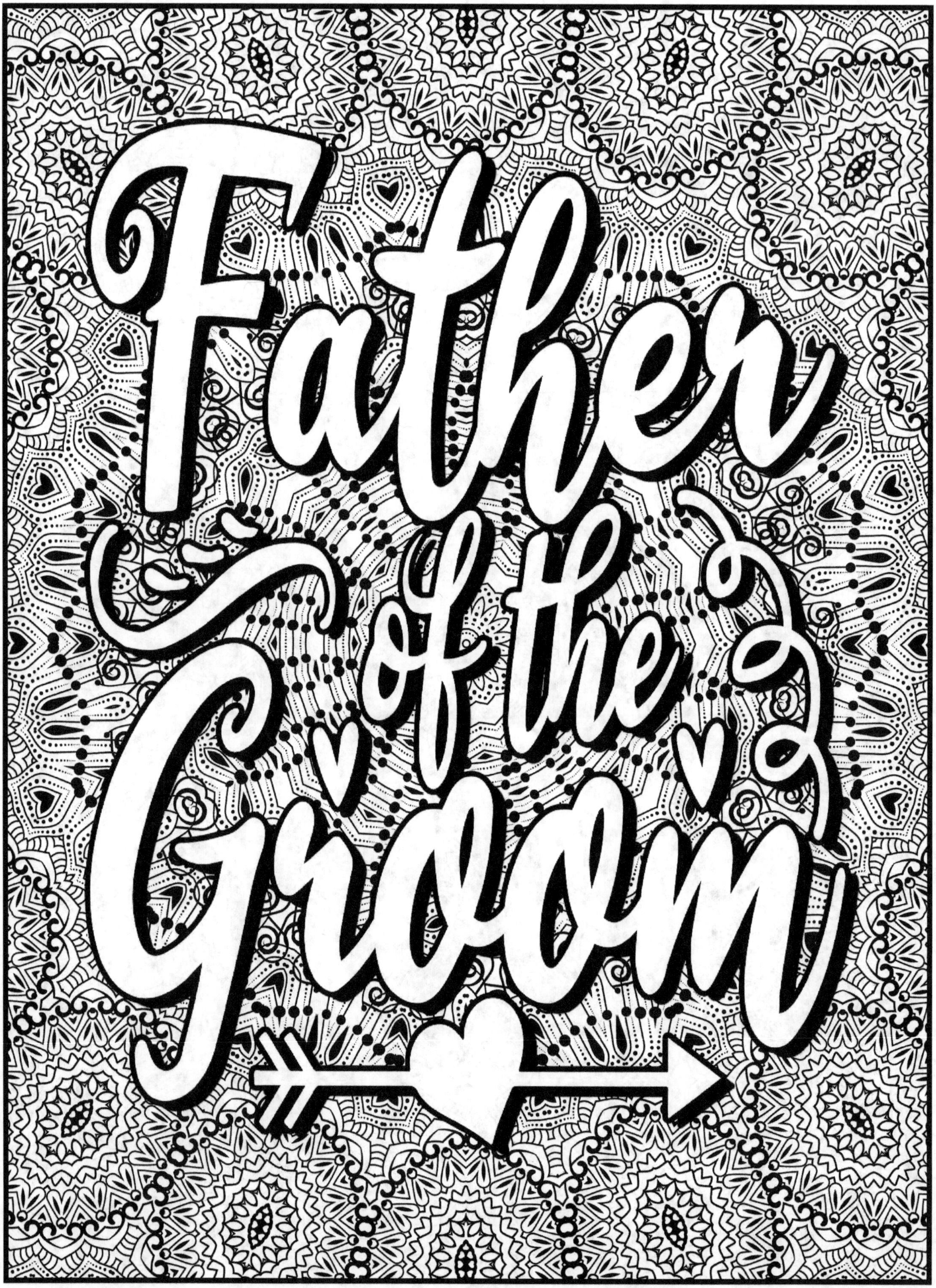
Father
of the
Groom

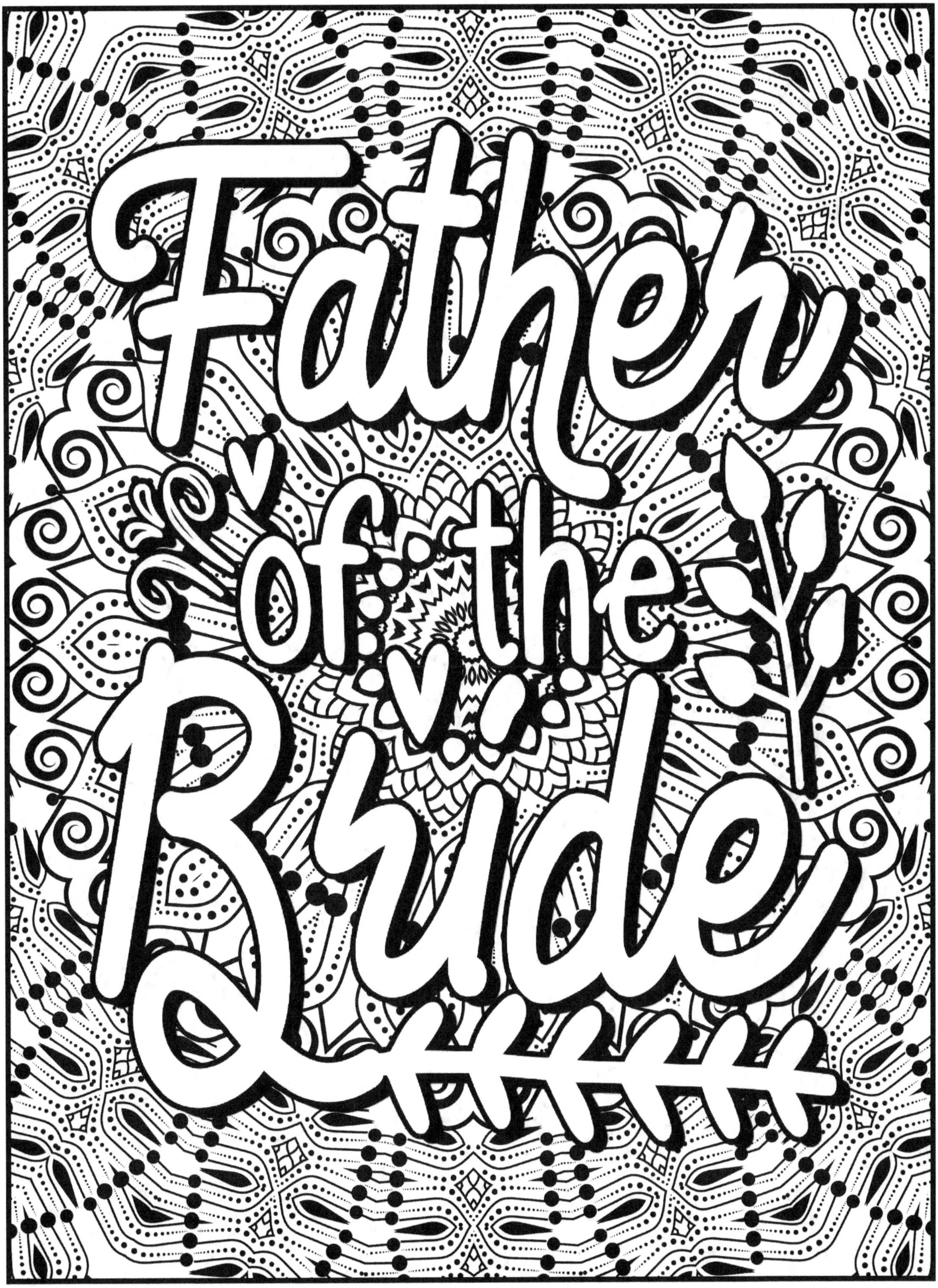
Father
of the
Bride

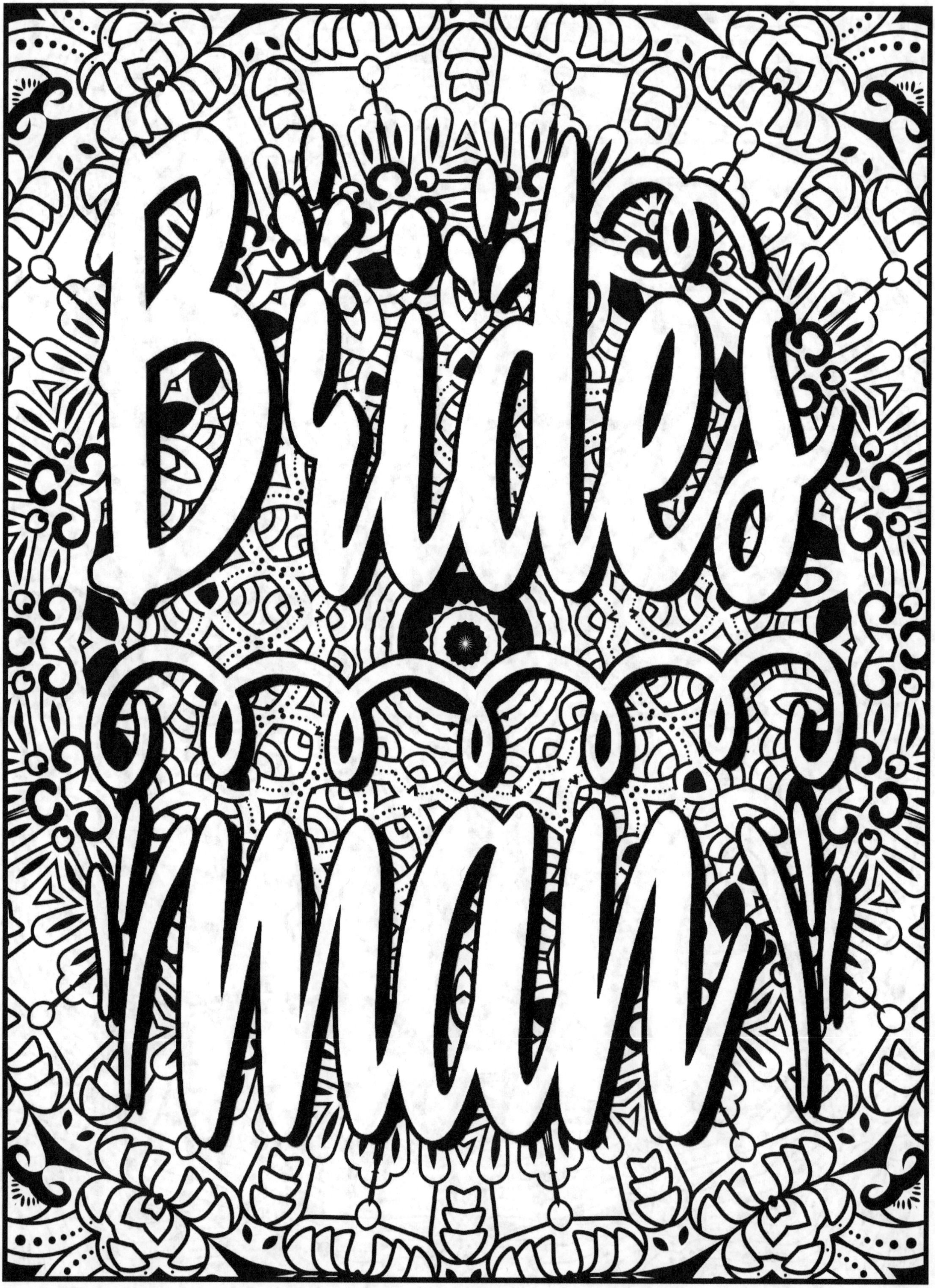
Brides
maid

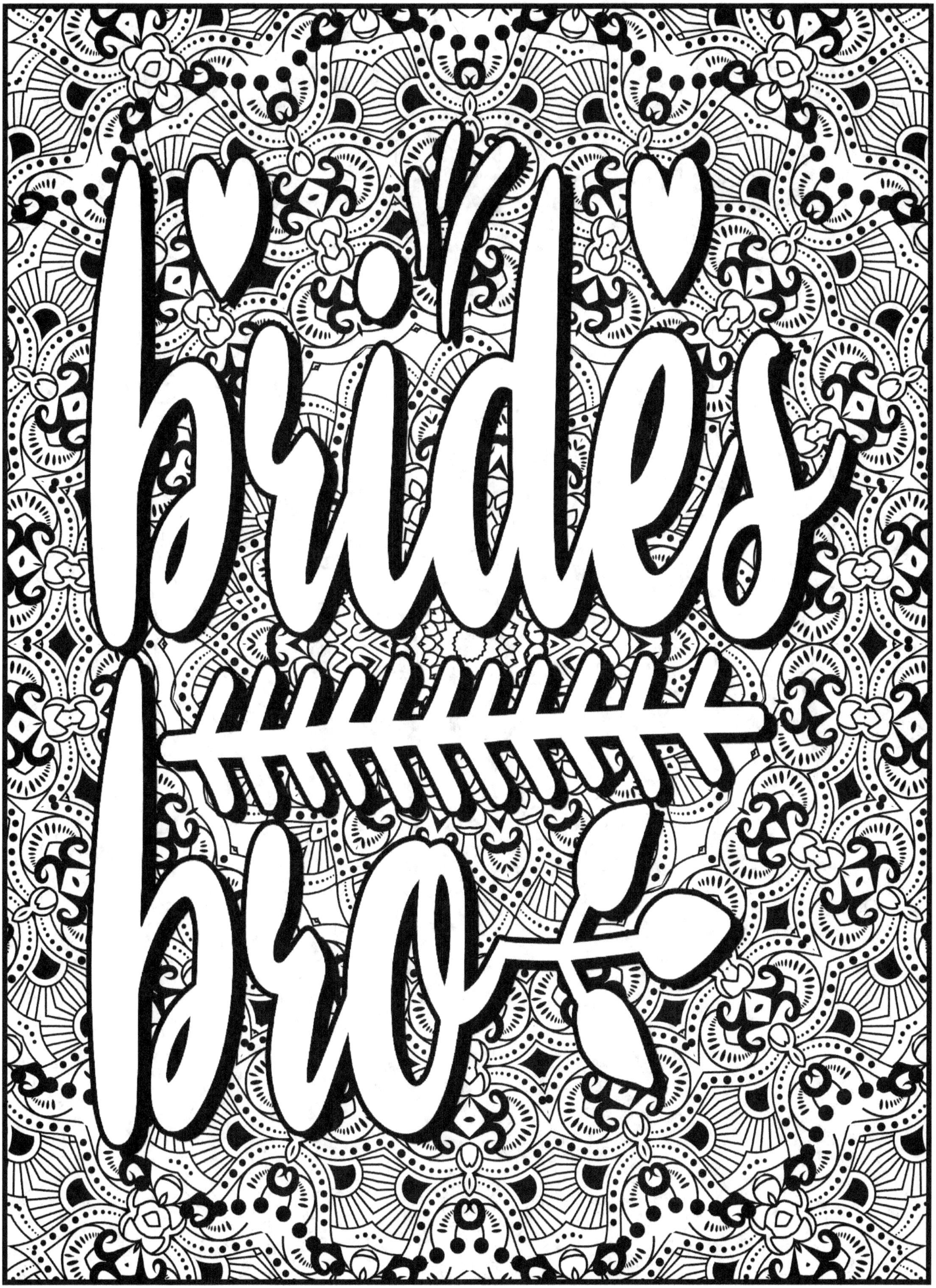
bride's
bro

Brides
BESTIES

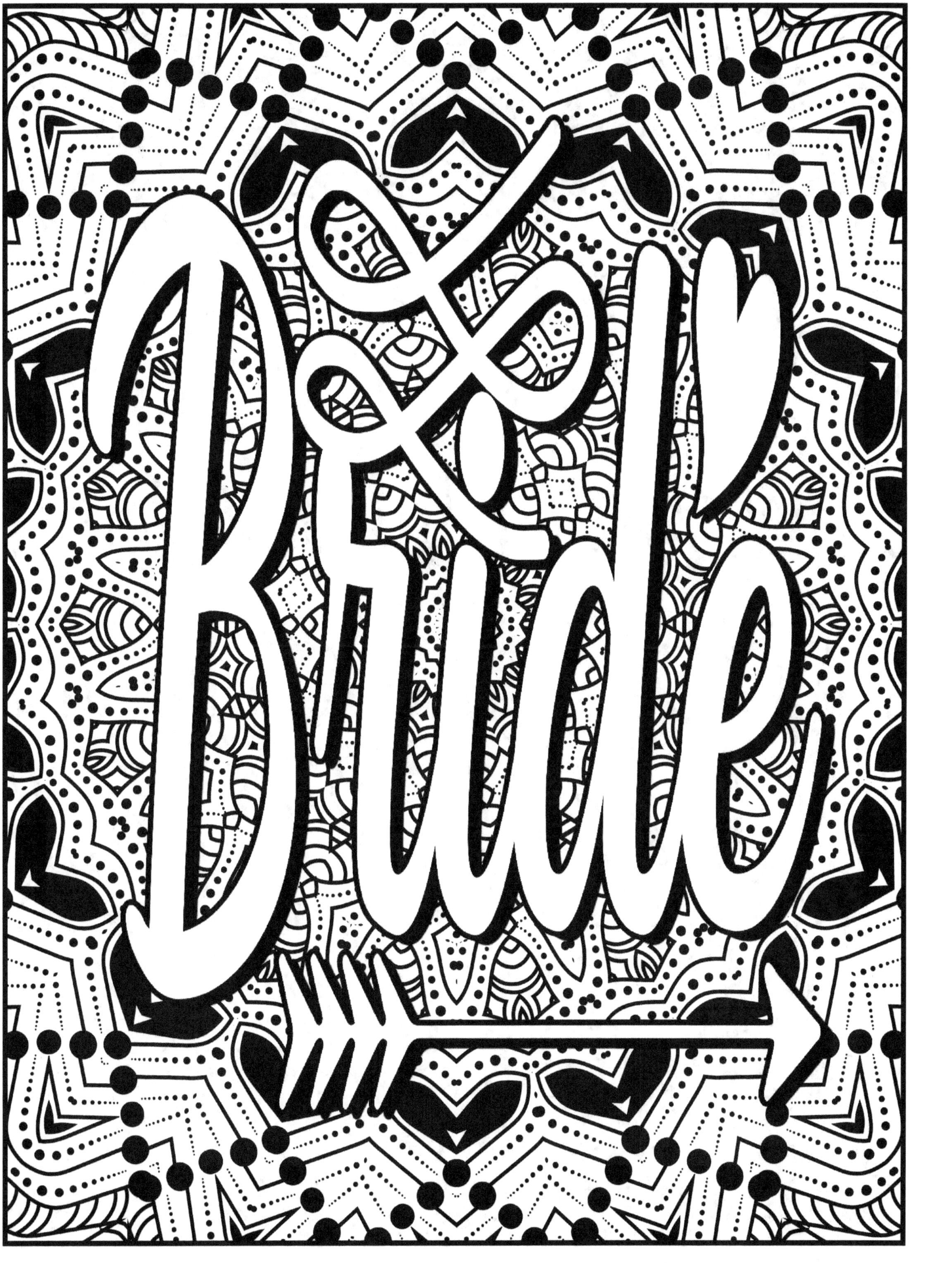
Bride

Ring
bearer

Green

junior
bridesmaid

grandma
of the
groom

Flower
girl

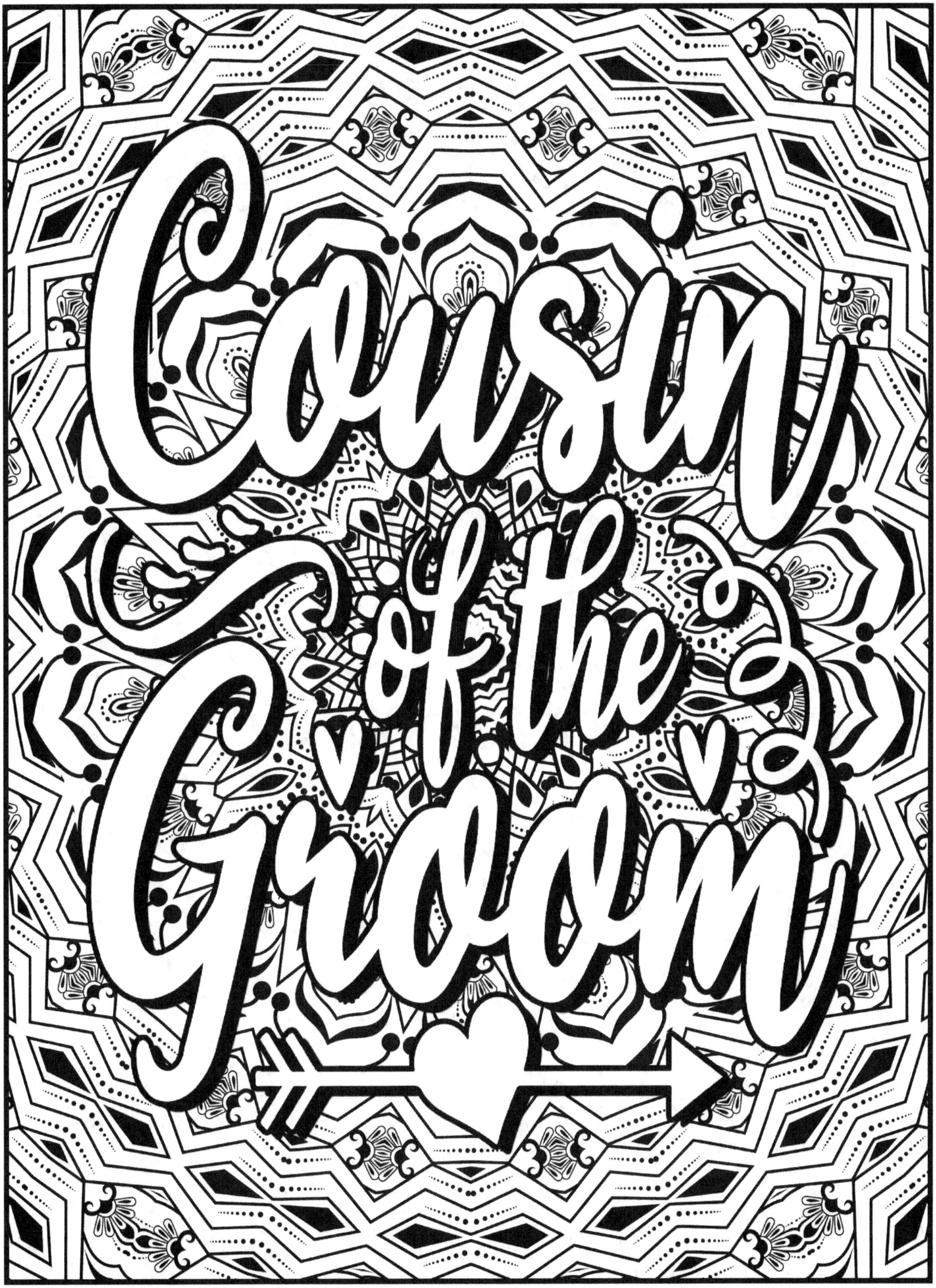
Cousin
of the
Groom

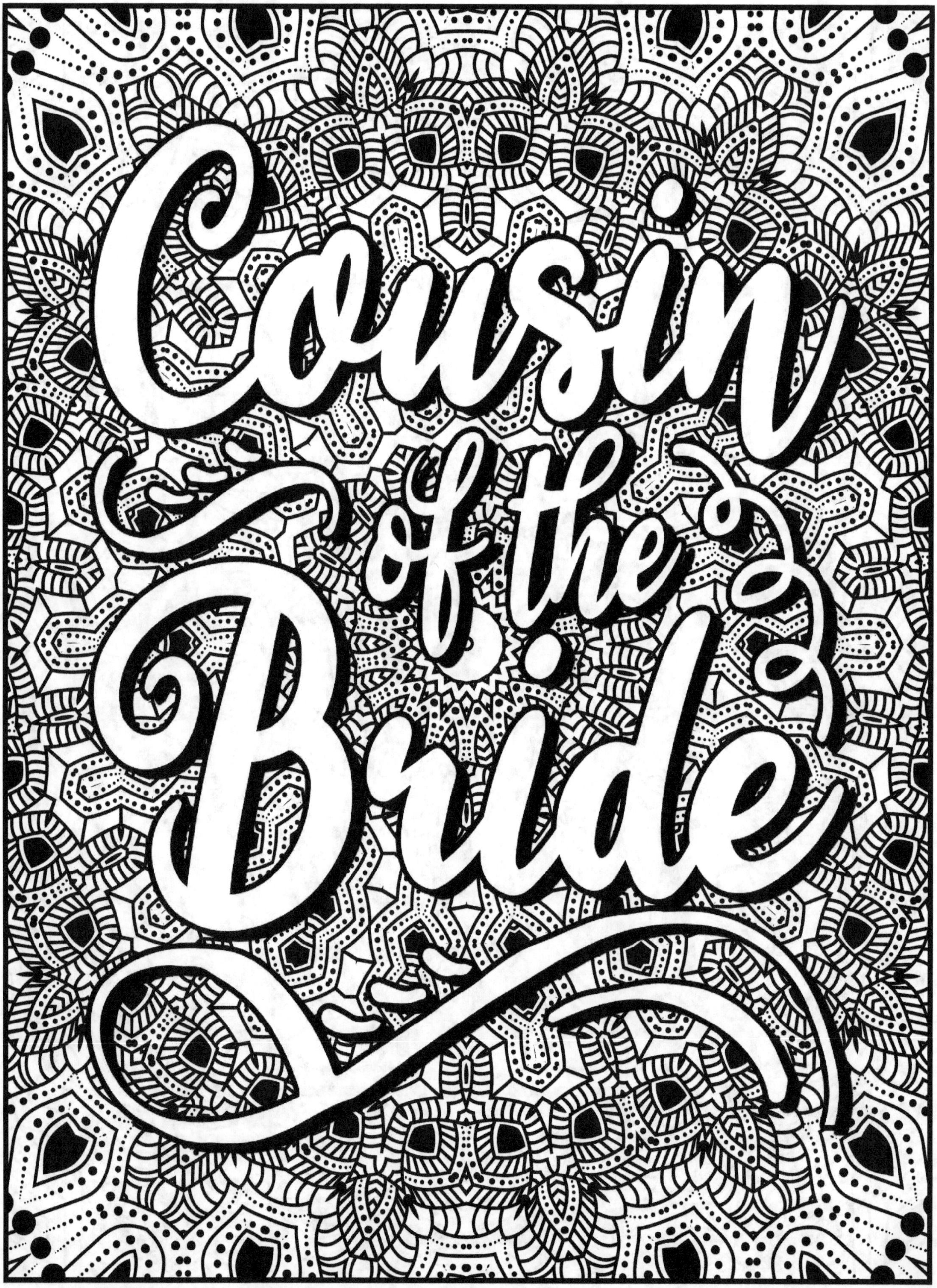
Cousin
of the
Bride

Cheers
to the
Future
mr+mrs

The
Bestman

The
BESTMAN

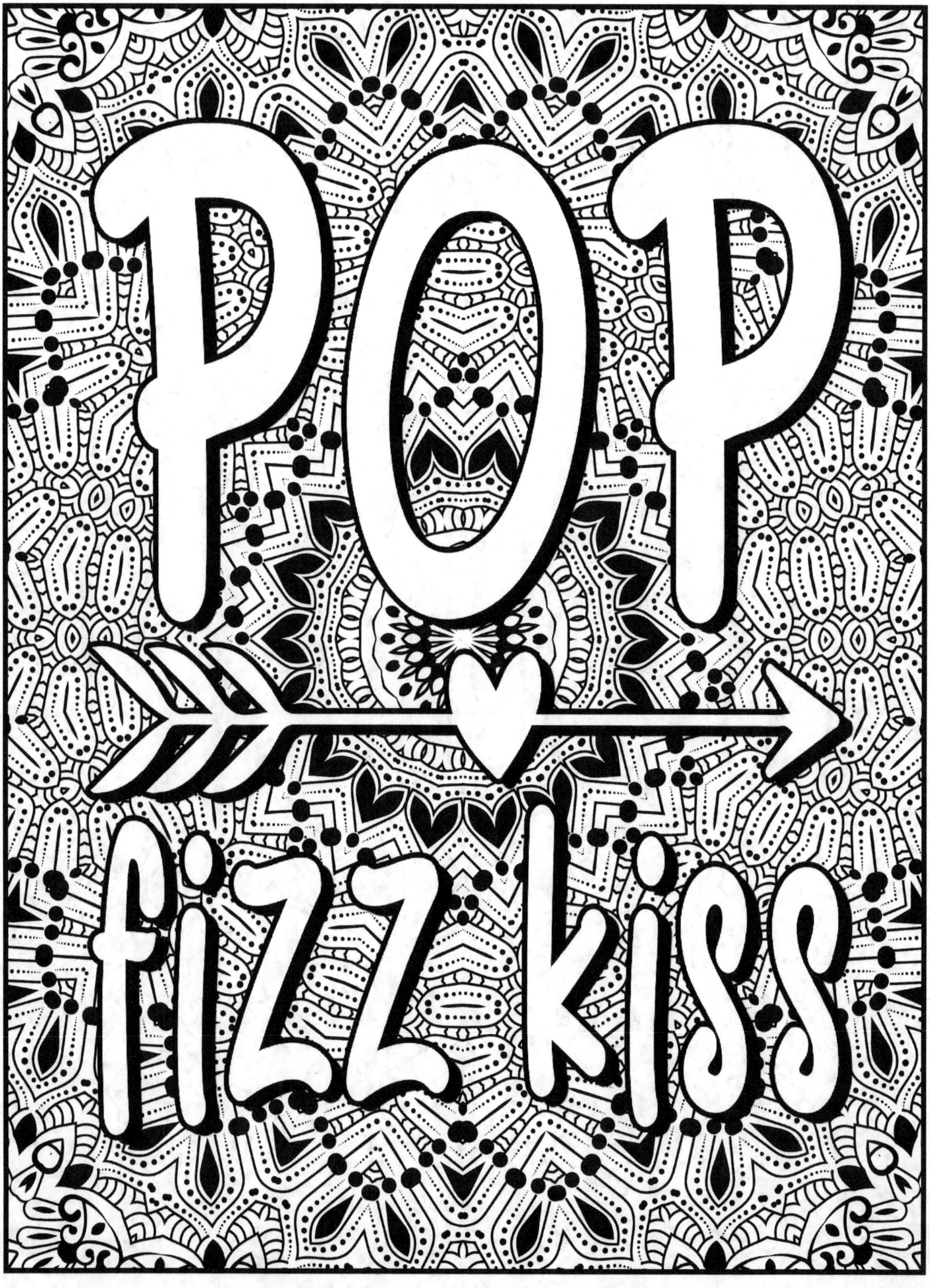
POP
fizz kiss

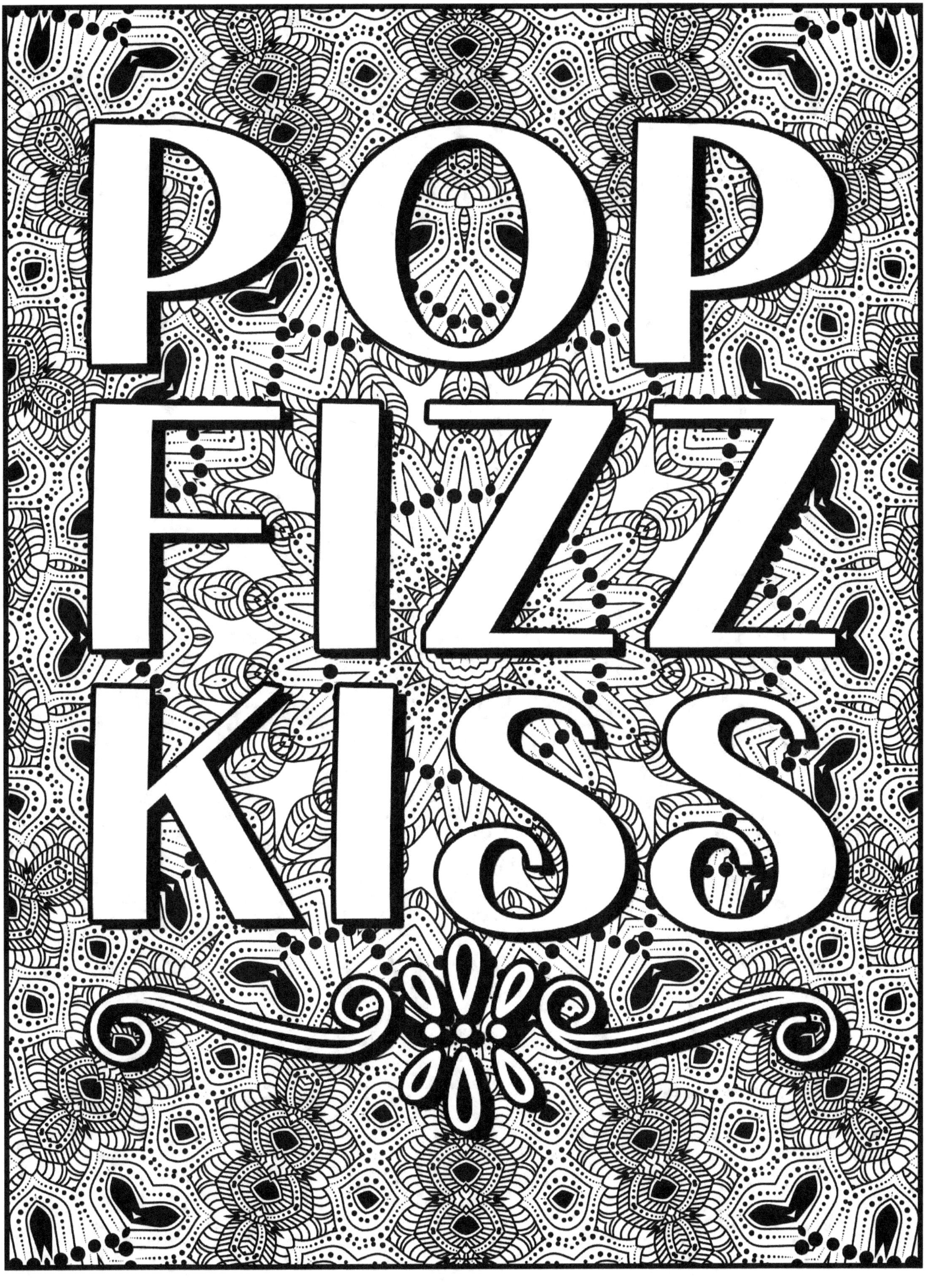
POP
FIZZ
KISS

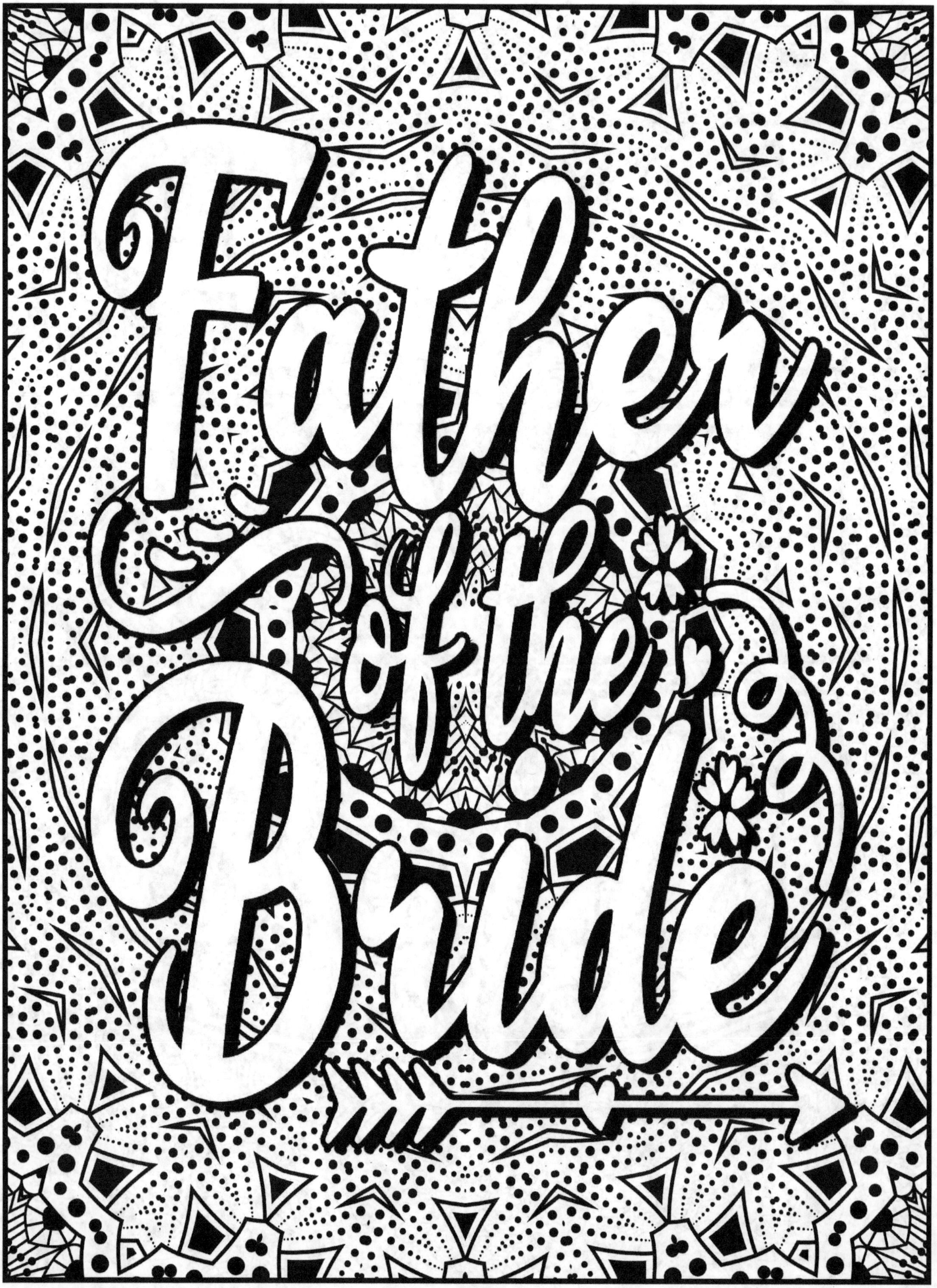
Father
of the
Bride

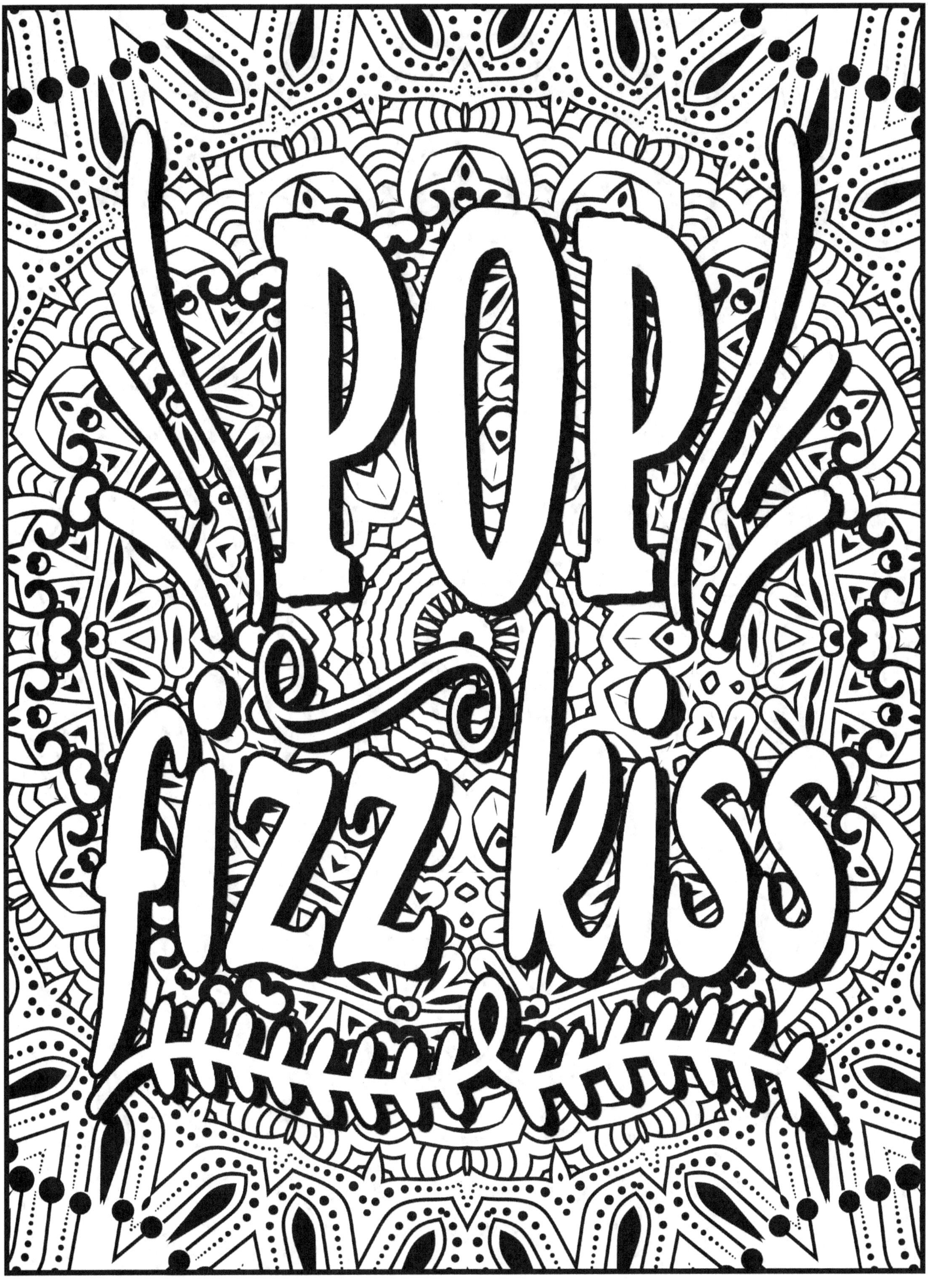
POP
fizz kiss

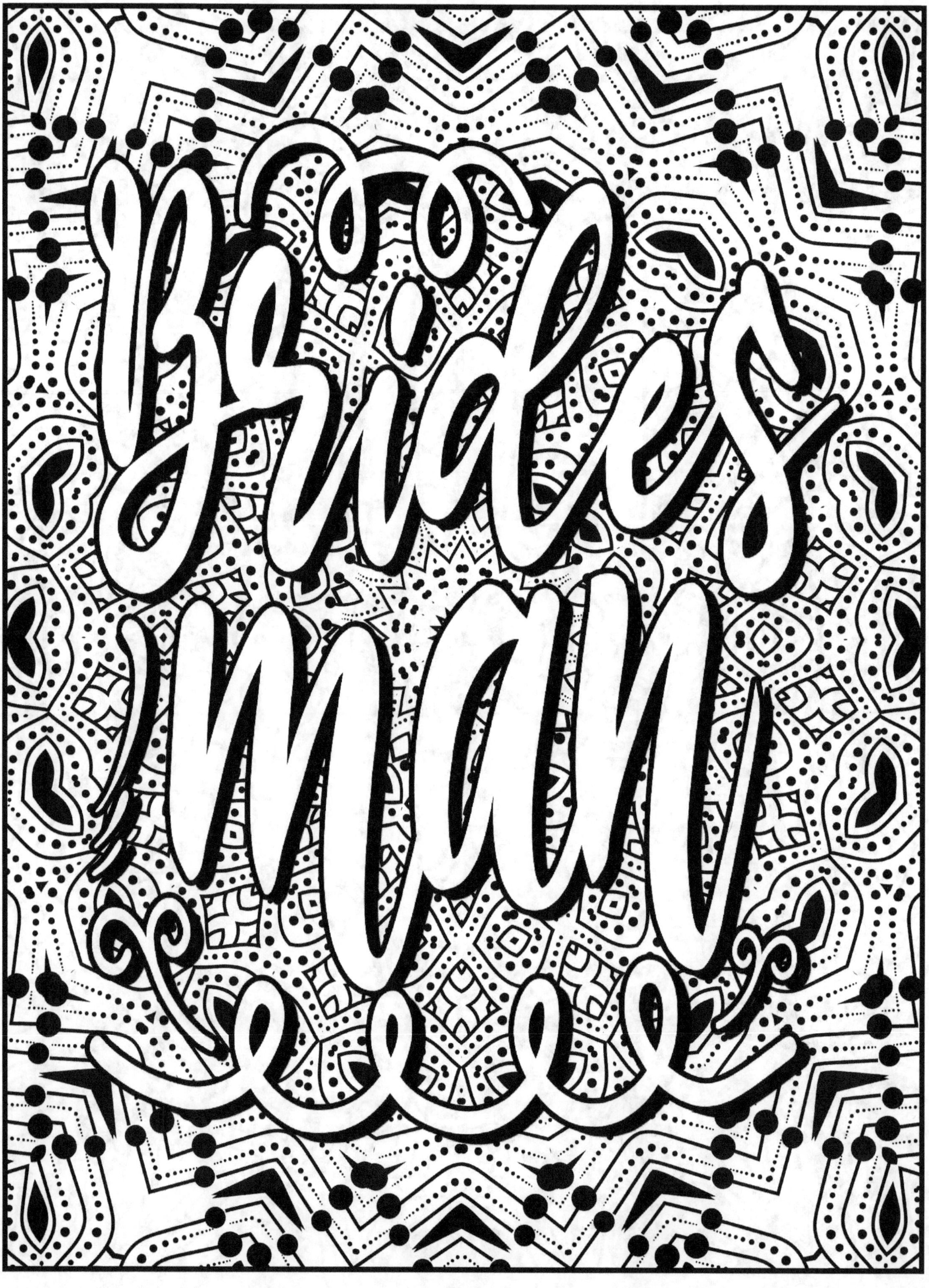
Brides
man

Bride's
MAID

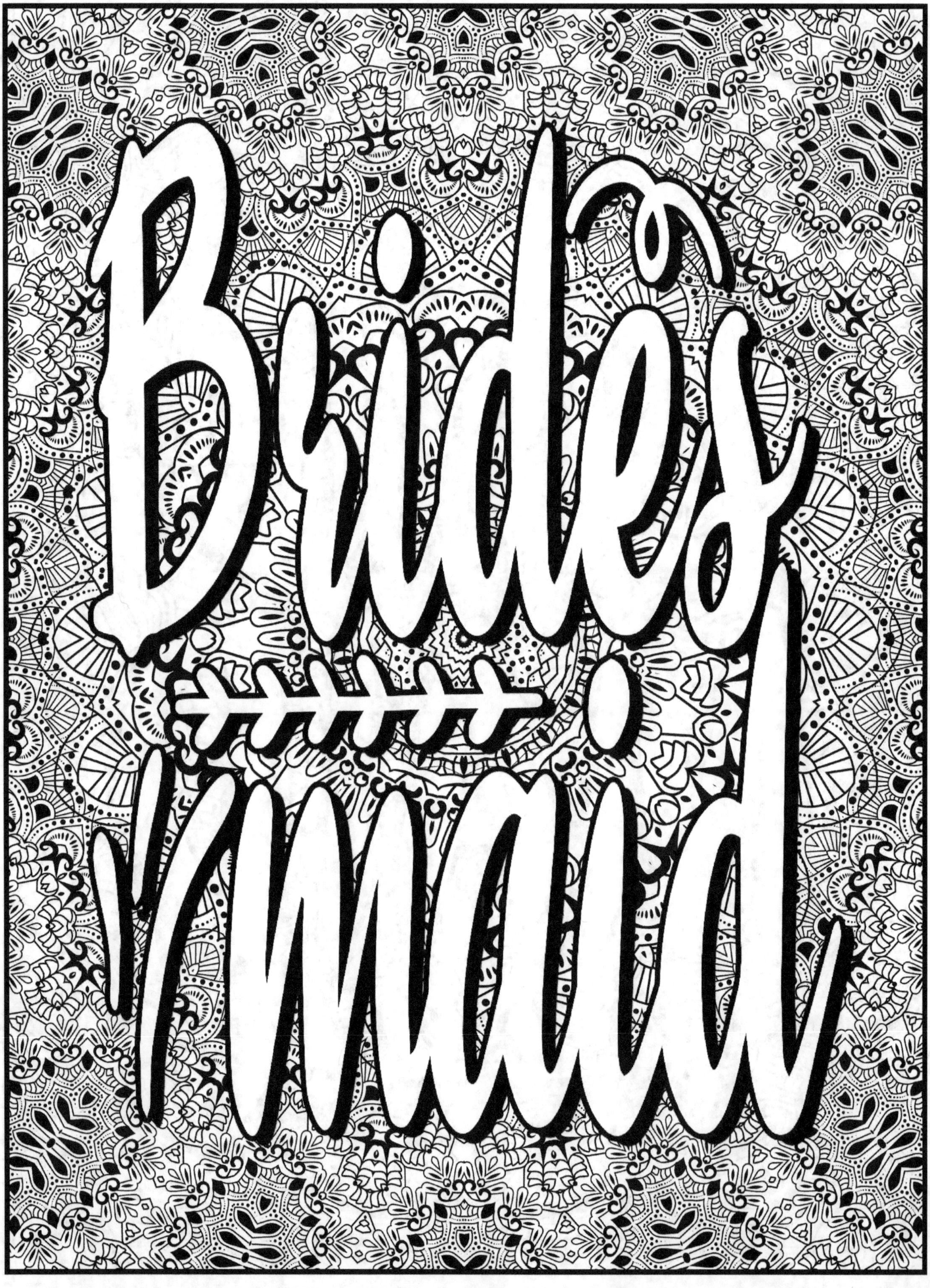
Brides
maid

Brides
Maid

Bride

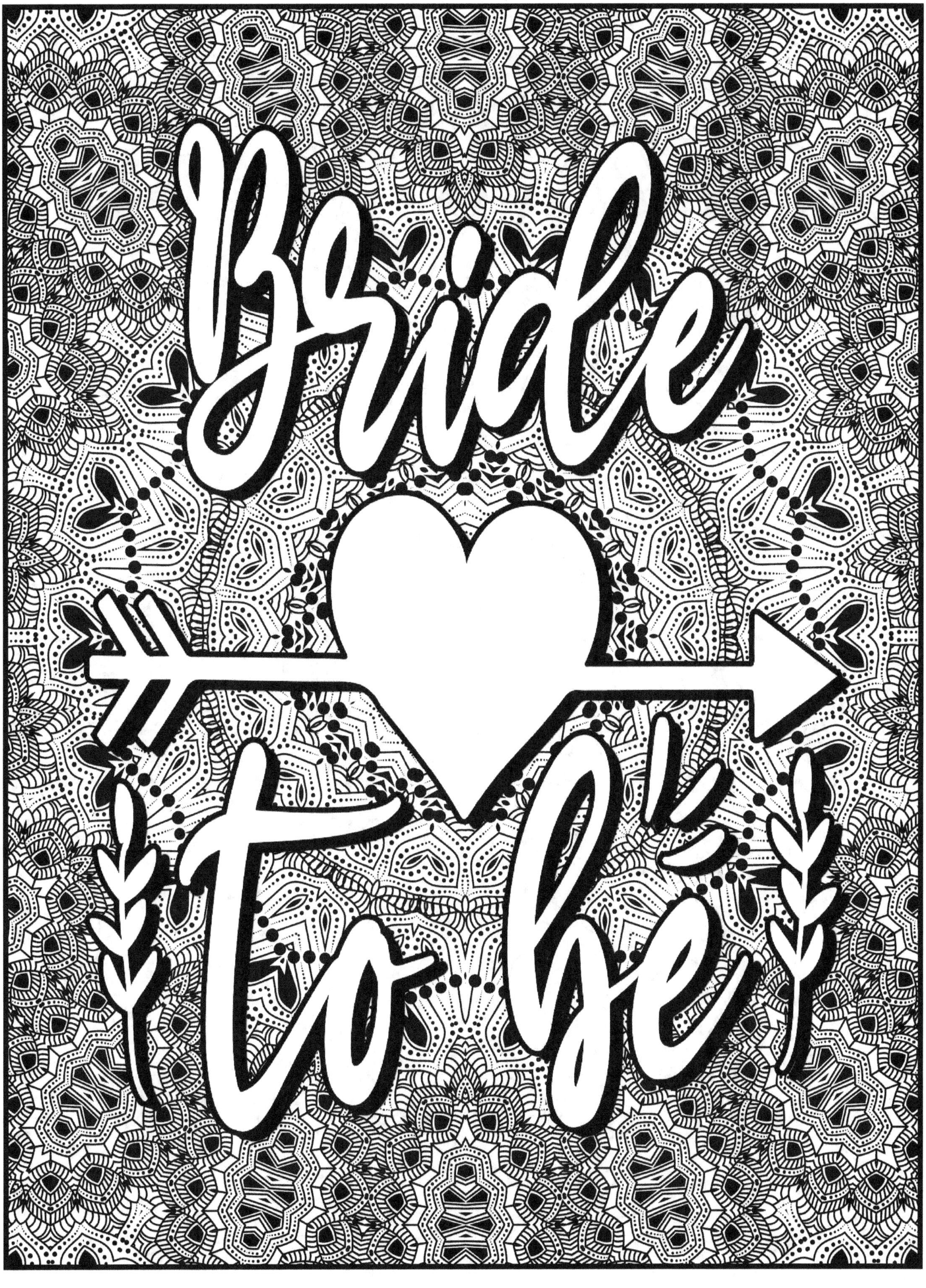
Bride
to be

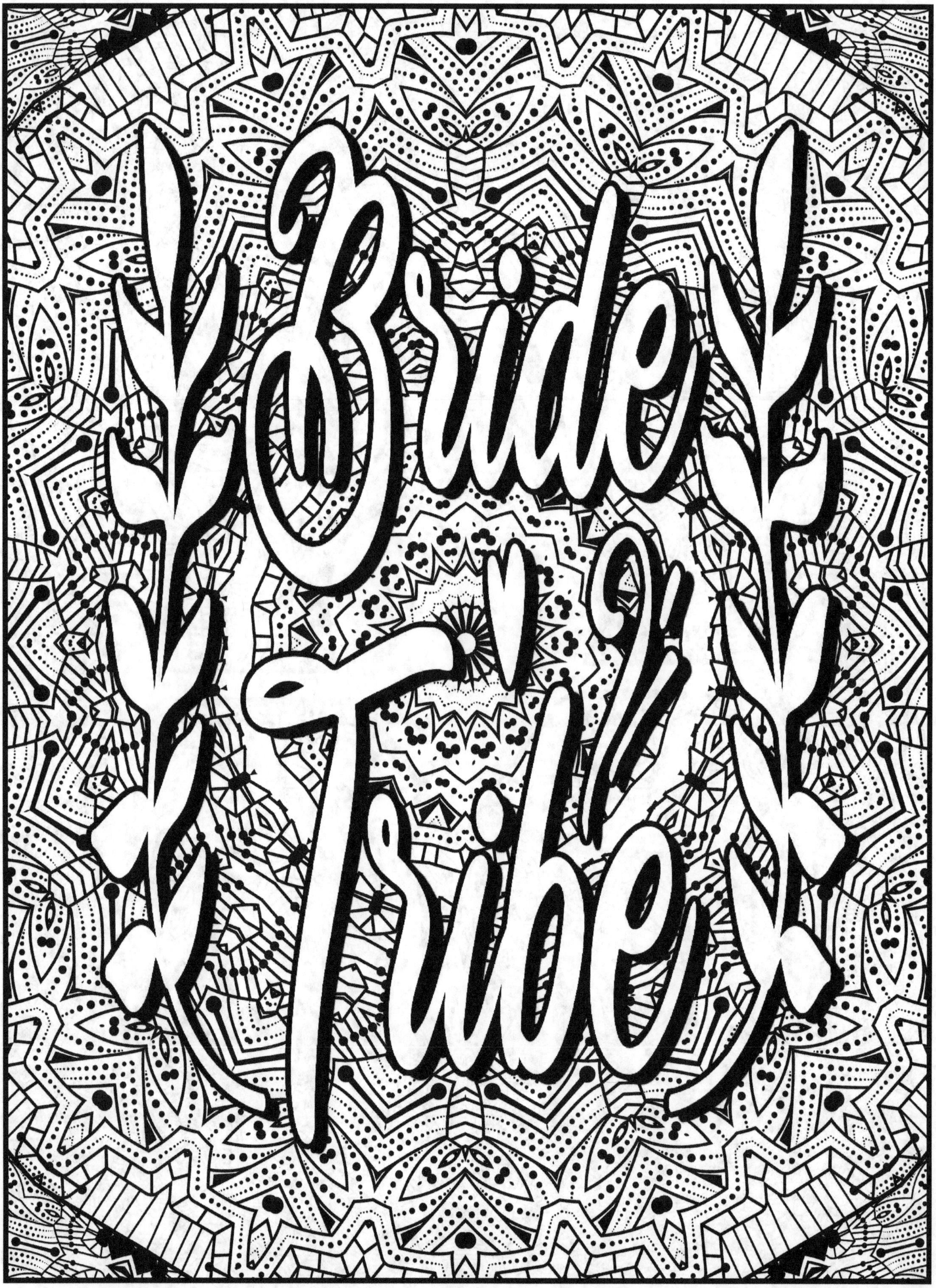
Bride
Tribe

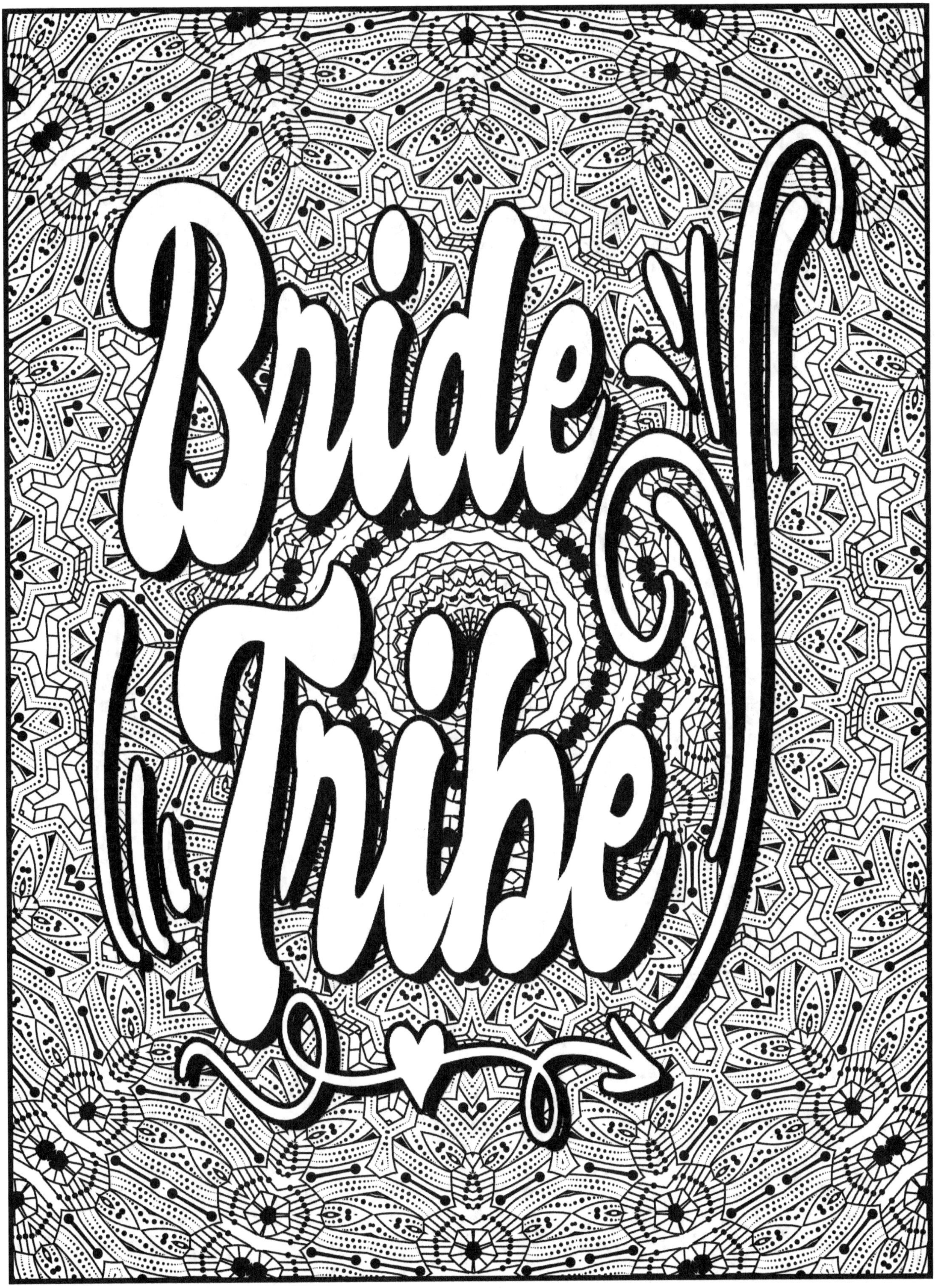
Bride
Tribe

Bride
ANNOUNCER

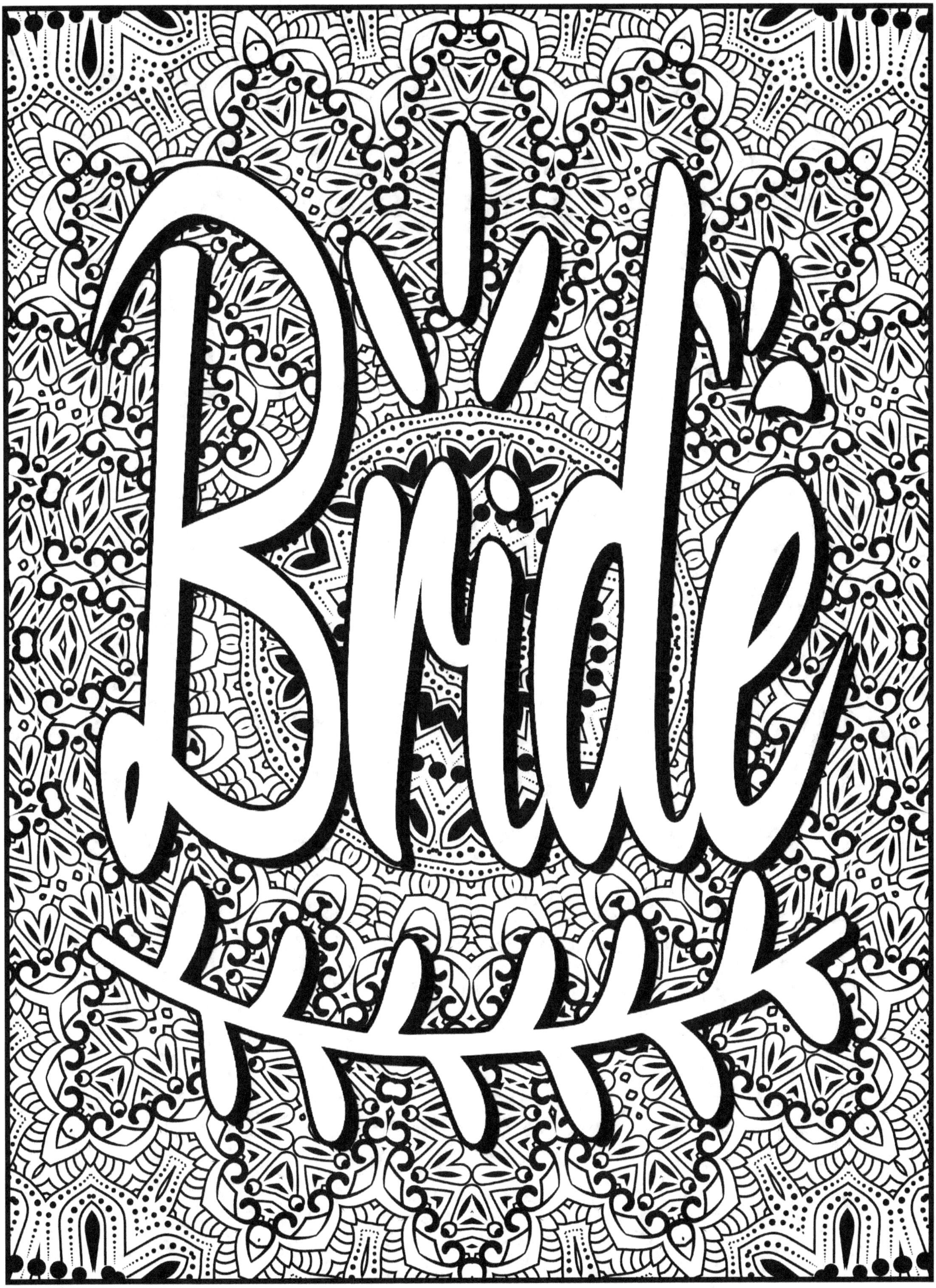
Bride

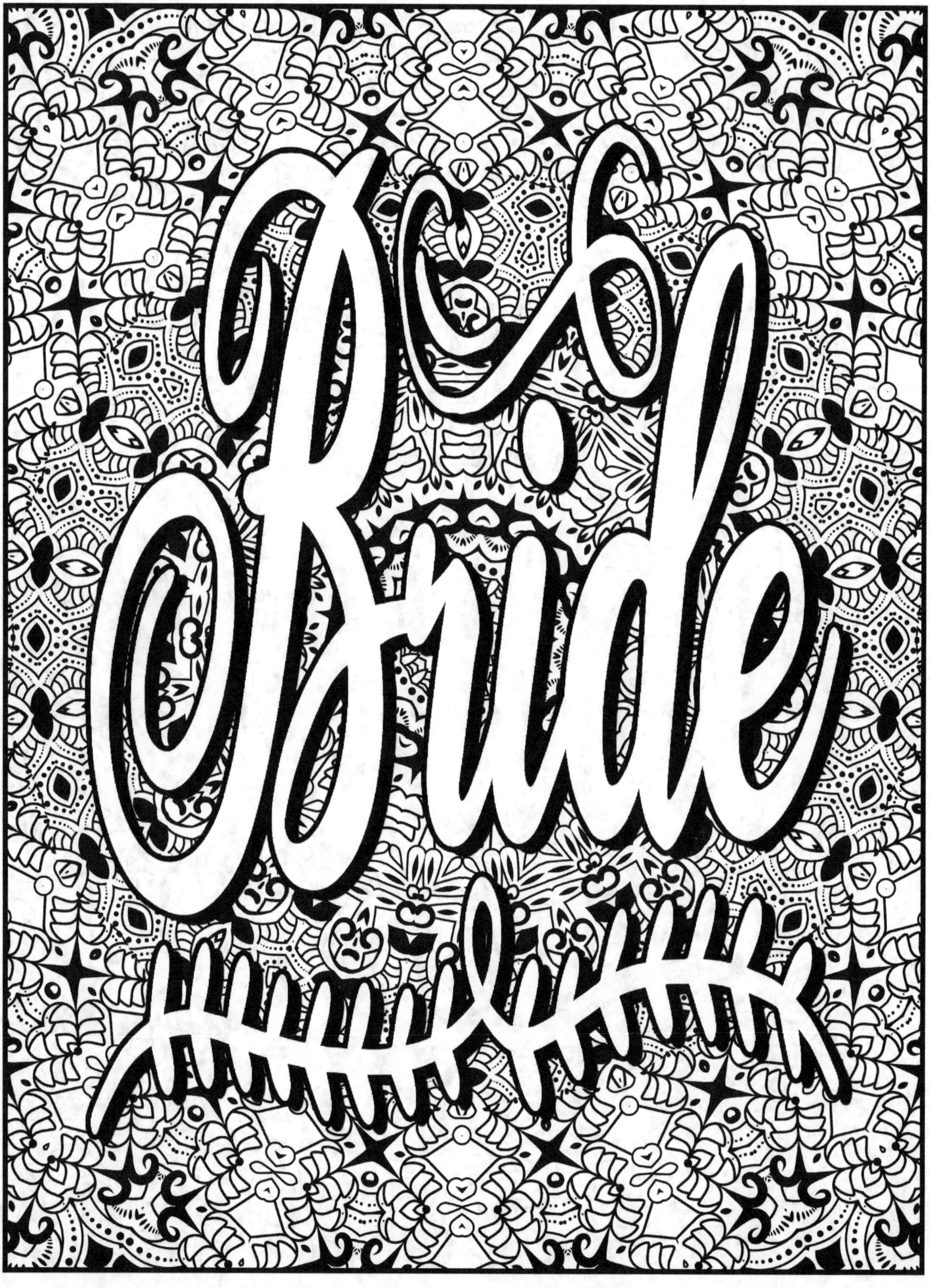
Bride

Bride

Bestie
of the
Bride

Bestie
OF THE
Bride

babe
OF
honor

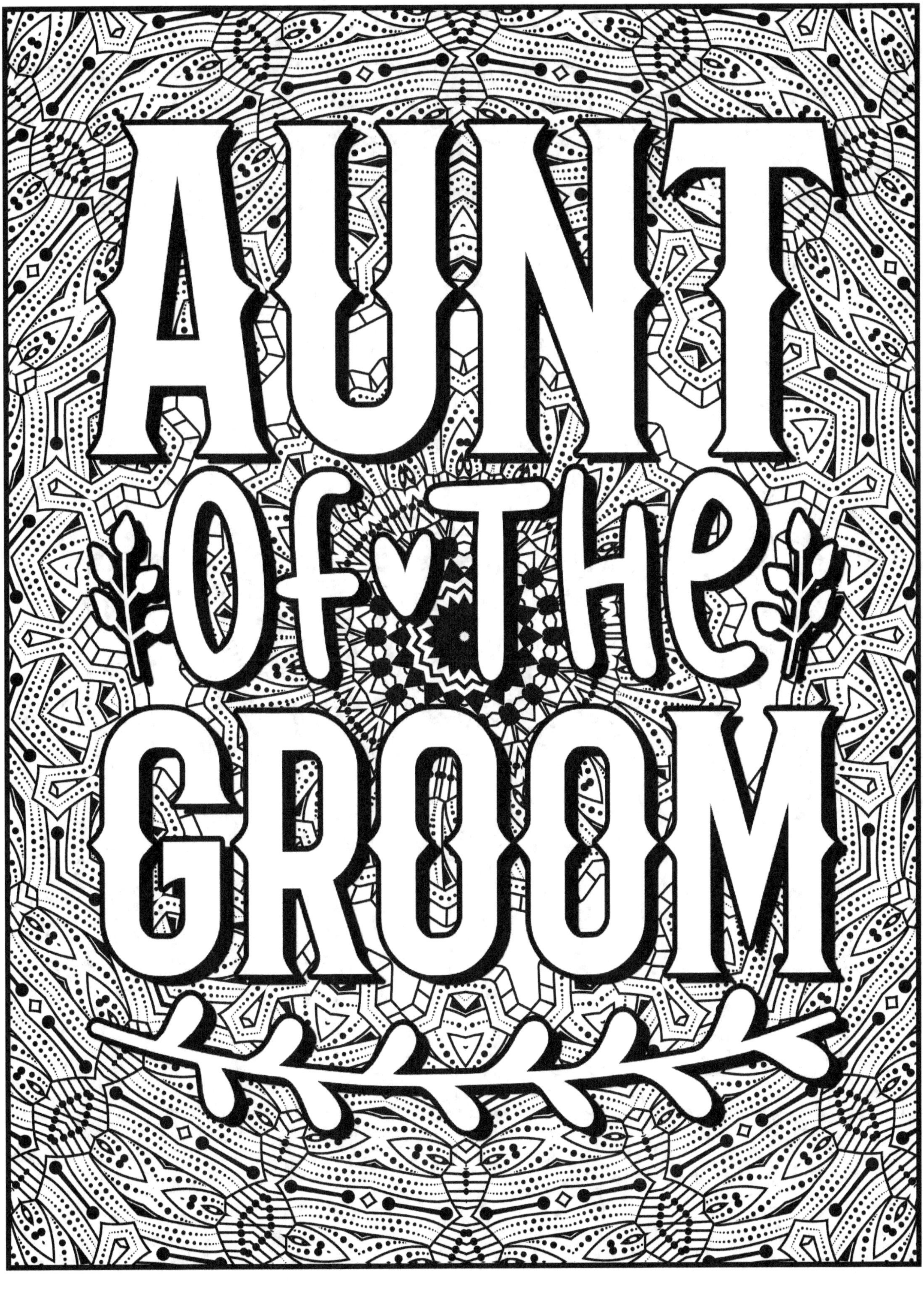
AUNT
of the
GROOM

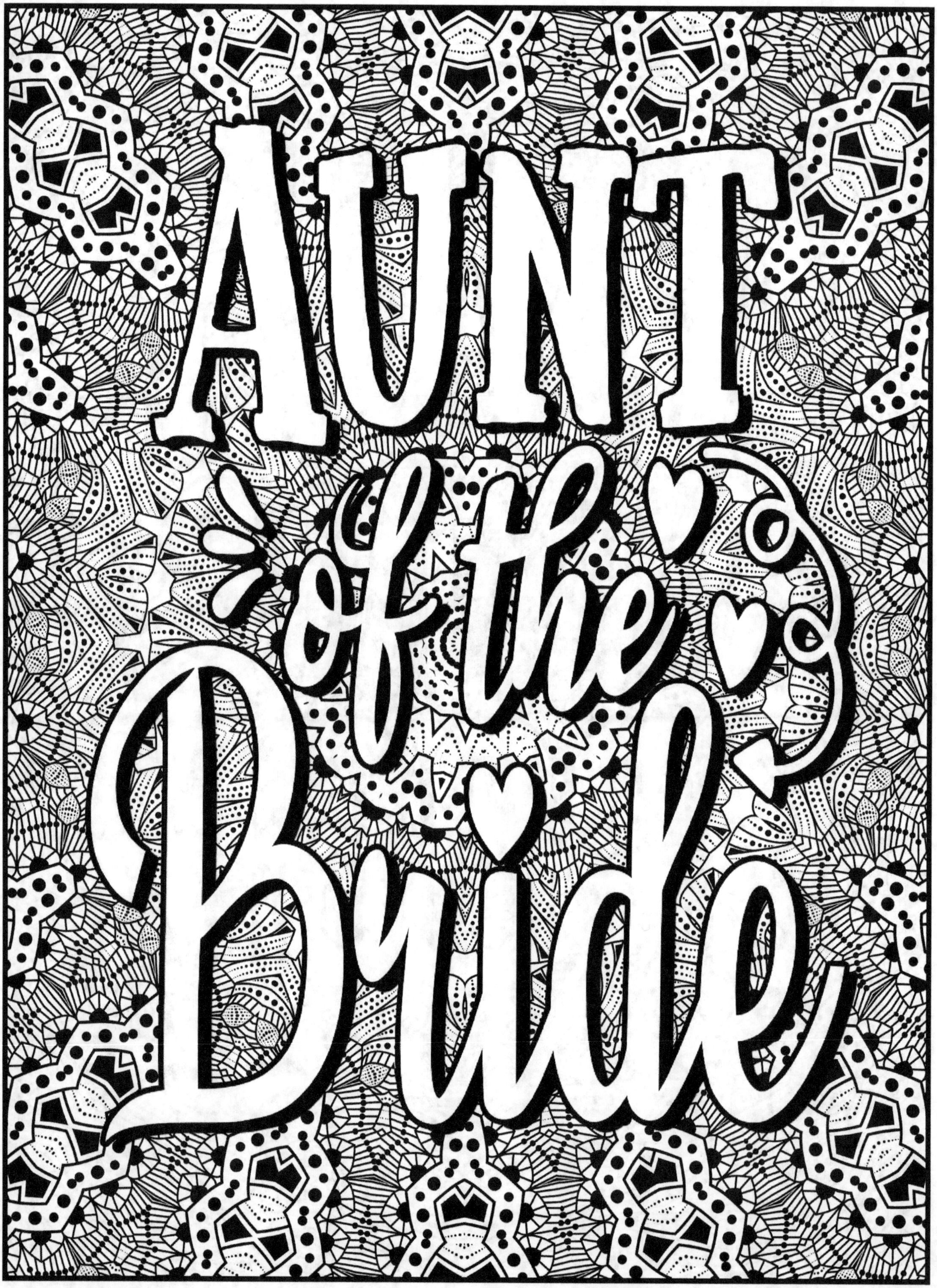
AUNT
of the
Bride

TEAM
Bride

Thankful for my tribe

Sweating
FOR THE
wedding

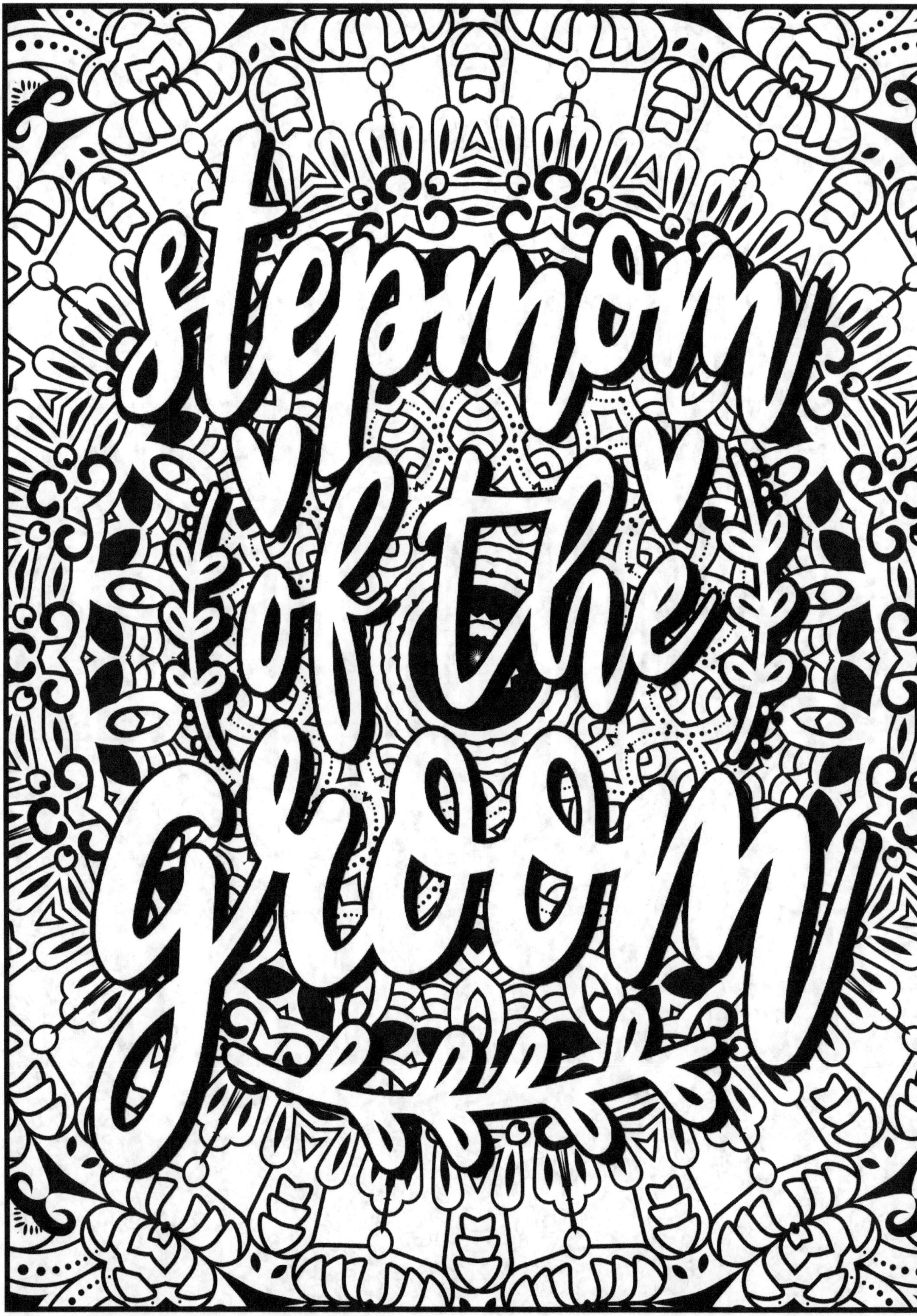
stepmom
of the
groom

stepmom
of the
bride

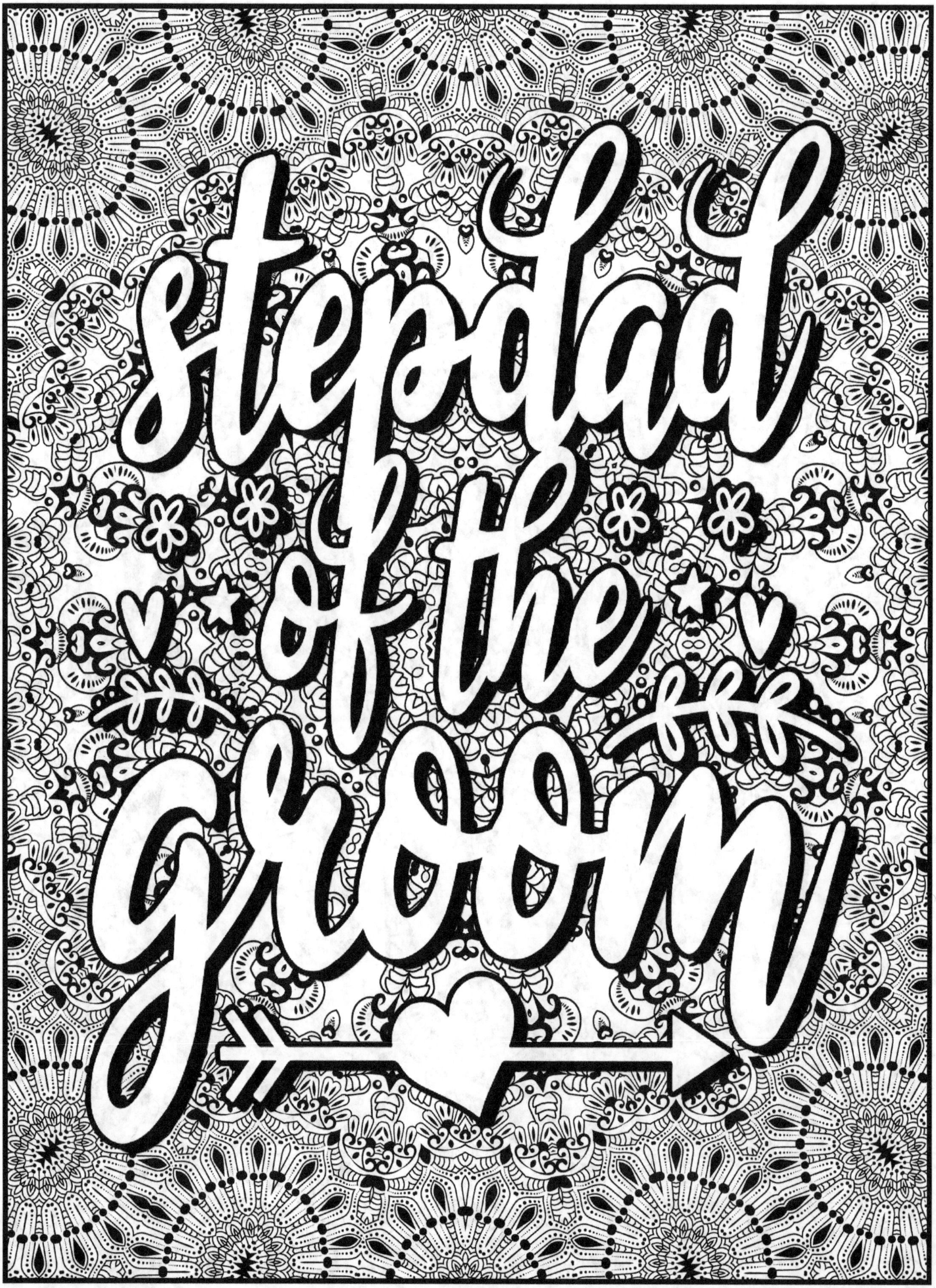
stepdad
of the
groom

sister
of the
groom

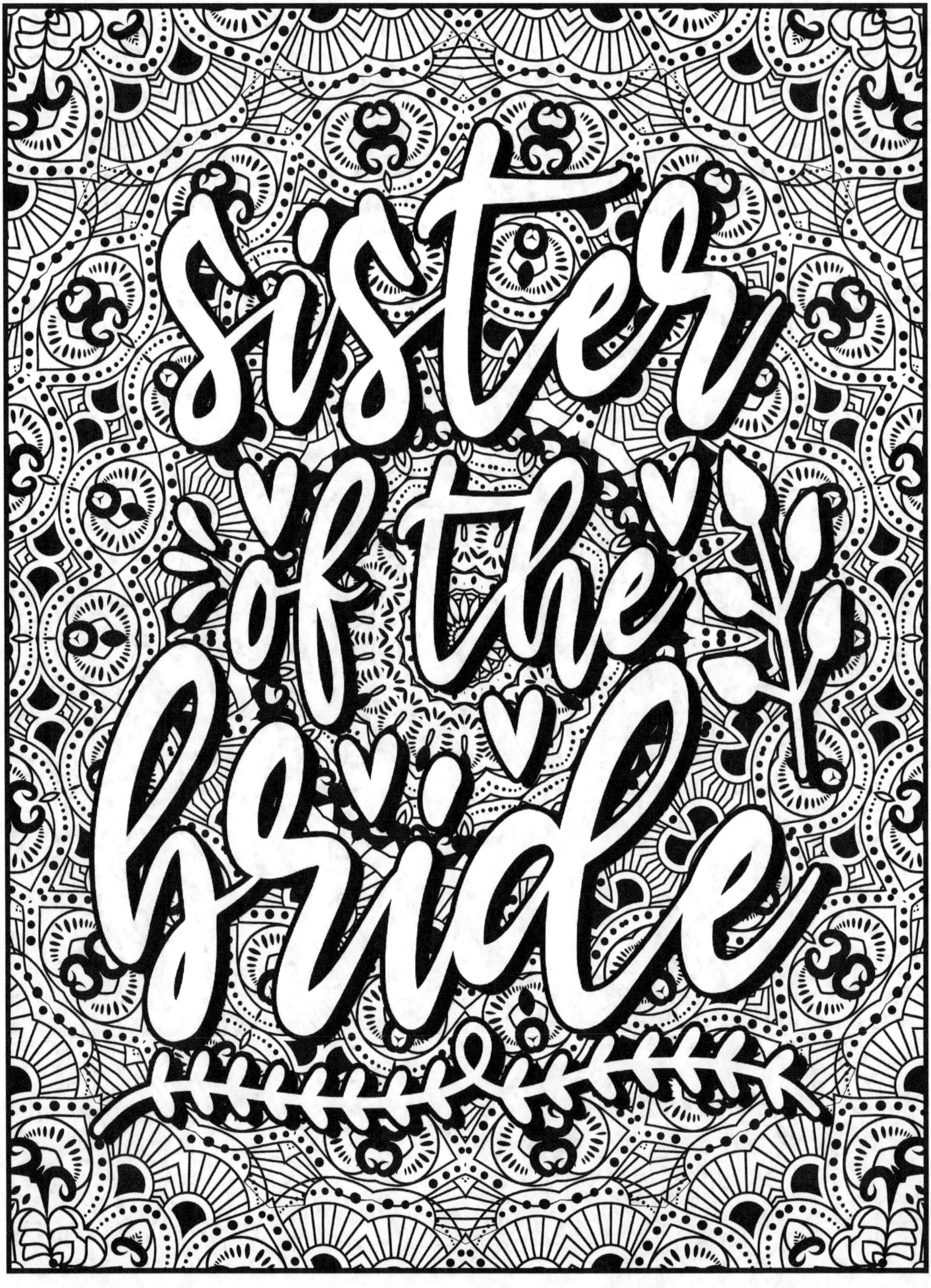
sister
of the
bride

Ring
bearer

RING.
Security

www.ingramcontent.com/pod-product-compliance
Lightning Source LLC
Chambersburg PA
CBHW062228220526
45471CB00009B/3388